Poetic Colors

Linda Diane Fay   Angelia Richhart   Amber Richhart

The Fay Family

Books

By

The Essence of a Pearl

The Sugar Orchard

Divinely Guided:

Faith, Love, Hope, Peace & joy

Lay Family Publishing

Poetic Colors

Copyright 2016 © Lay Family Publishing

Authors: Linda Diane Lay, Angelia Richhart, Amber Richhart,

Lay Family & Royal House of Normandy Royal Lay Family

All rights reserved. Published in the United States - Lay Family Publishing,
Originally published, printed & manufactured in the United States.
Lay Family Publishing © No portion of this book may be reproduced in any form without
written permission from the publisher or authors, except as permitted by U.S. copyright
law. While every precaution has been taken in the preparation of this book, the publisher
assumes no responsibility for errors or omissions, or for damages resulting from the use of
the information contained herein.

Tittle: Poetic Colors
Author Names: Linda Diane Lay, Angelia Richhart, Amber Richhart, Lay Family &
Royal House of Normandy Royal Lay Family
Description: Volume of free verse Poetry
Identifiers:
(Hardcover ISBN: 978-1-300-48049-5)
(Paperback ISBN: 978-1-300-21550-9) (Paperback ISBN: 9798223467441)
(E-Book ISBN: 9798201844325)

Subjects: Classification BISAC (North America)

POE001000   POETRY / Anthologies (multiple authors)
POE005010   POETRY / American / General
POE023030   POETRY / Subjects & Themes / Animals & Nature
POE024000   POETRY / Women Authors

Lay Family Publishing
Published & Printed in the United States of America

10   9   8   7   6   5   4   3   2   1

Table of Contents

Loving Embrace

The moon is at its highest peak tonight,
with a shadowy light gleaming down.

Piercing through my window and my silk laced
gown.

I was in hopes to find my lover,
but he could not be found.

But the hint of honey suckles still lingered all
around.

As I slowly walked across the floor,
to latch thy swaying door.

I could feel a cool breeze rushing in,
from the night's roaring ocean winds.

I felt your gentle touch,
which made me turn around.

As you grasped me with your loving arms,
I knew I had been found.

Love of God

For she always treasured love and all that it
could give.

It could even replenish a soul's will to truly
live.

For love covers a multitude of sins we always
bear.

The beautiful thing about love is that it
neither judges nor does it care.

It never cares about
our mistakes, our imperfections or our flaws.

Love is always there to catch us,
when we happen to fall.

Love is truly beautiful,
I hope you get to see.
The way God intended love to always be.

The Season's Secrets

The crumbling leaves fell upon the forest
floor,
to the sun's glistening waves upon the ocean
shore.
From the snow-glistening flakes falling from
the sky,
to the warmth of a spring day bearing new
life.
From the warm embracing breeze of
summer's eve,
to the colored filled foliage falling from the
trees.
From the glistening dew resting upon a blade
of grass,
to the sound of the oceans roar
always remembering its past.
From the peaks of the highest mountains
simmering secrets,
to the sandy floors unkept secrets.

A Summer's Bliss

The day lilies and their yellow blossom
blooms,
called the hummingbirds with their sweet
perfume.

As the aroma of sweetness and beauty filled all
the spring days,
you could imagine how I wish spring could so
desperately stay.

The hummingbirds are always humming with
delight and bliss,
I know spring too; they would surely miss.

But spring soon fades into a summery bliss,
and you'll receive summers sweetness
you won't want to miss.

Rose Blossoms

The roses with their alluring aroma slowly climb
up the garden's gates,
twirling and twisting their vines as if this was
their destined fate.

Reaching for the sky and the sun's warming
rays,
so they could delicately bloom,
and you could hopelessly gaze.

Knowing that their beauty is untouched by
man,
but understanding the seed of truth that all
miracles are by God's hand.

The Old Oak Tree

Life is so beautiful and yet so free,
when I dream and reminisce under
the old oak tree.

As I grip the chains upon thy swing,
I press back and lean in
to begin to swing.

I remember all the moments
I once have had.

With all the laughter and joy,
my heart was glad.

I look at today and where I am,
understanding life, love, and
the simplicity
of man.

Yearning Heart

Some hearts yearn for more than this life can
truly give.

Not materialistic things,
but to truly live.

We bridge the gap between
our mind and our heart.

Never knowing the full distance,
this is what sets us apart.

There are three things that are true about
love.
It takes all your body, soul, and mind
to fully love.

Without these three things,
there is nothing to be gained.

For why do you think falling in love always
ends in so much pain?

Blue Array

I walked along the seashore
in the coolness of dawn's first light.

I could see the waves crashing
with their grip held so tight.

Within the waters of the ocean,
there is a blue array.

I could feel the emotions of the ocean,
as it began a new day.

Always knowing and always turning tides.

It seemed to hold so many secrets,
you only got to wish you knew in time.

A Love Song

I hear the sparrows chirping their sweet spring
chimes,
as I walk through the rose garden
that's covered in vines.

The sparrows and doves have found their mate,
and are nesting nearby the garden's gates.

I see the sun rising,
as I look toward the east.

Feeling the warmth of the sun upon my
unsandaled feet.

I followed a dirt path that led to the fountains.

As I could see in the distance,
the earth's beautiful array of mountains.

Springs Joyous Songs

The roses and the lilies always sleep all winter
long,
resting their beauty before spring sings its joyous
song.
While the cardinals and the blue jays never tend
to migrate south,
they always tend to wait old man winter out.
But as the winter passes and the snow soon turns
to rain.
We always tend to get saddened by April's rainy
days.
But those clouds will soon pass,
as they never seem to last too long.
Then we will get to enjoy all of spring's joyous
songs.
For the flowers will be in bloom,
to brighten up your day.
Then all the beautiful spring creatures
will be out to play.

Garden of Your Mind

A farmer sows so many seeds,
and if they fall on fertile soil they will grow
indeed.

Whether it's a beautiful rose

or

thistles and thorns.

What you water with your mind,
is what your heart adorns.

Speak from the Heart

Why are there so many regrets that live in our
hearts?
When couples first meet nothing can tear them
apart.

As time goes by,
they slowly drift apart.

Perhaps it's from the wedges they created
with the hateful words that they say.

As time goes by,
everything seems to fade away.

Maybe it could've been different,
if only they had chosen loving words to say.

Always speak from the heart
and
not from hate.

Life's too short to regret what we say.

Grandfather Clock

What is Time?

But a passing of our momentary moments.

We cannot help but count our time on the hands
of a clock.
Wishing it by,
even though it never really stops.

We wish it by,
through the hardest of our times.
Always asking the question of
Why? Why? Why?

But when we are happy and our lives are going
great,
you never really ponder the question of your fate.

Only in those moments do you feel weak and
alone.
Is when you sit, and you ponder.
Are you really alone?

Eternal Flame

The sweet tender kiss of a love so dearly missed,

To the poetic passions of a love not fully expressed.

From the heartfelt warmth of a handheld
kiss,
to the unshaken foundation of love's
sheer bliss.

From a lover's eternal flame
to
the heartache of a love that was lost,
all-consuming dull pain.

From being so blissfully young and naïve,
to never fully understanding why love
makes us grieve.

From being in an all-consuming love
worthwhile,
to engaging in loves sweet sympathetic
smiles.

True Loves Test

She loved the idea of love and all that it
entailed.

She even loved the old stories of love like the
unforgotten fairytales,
not because they were perfect and not because
they were real.

But
because they represented a love that never
seemed to fail.

She never believed love was perfect,
but she did believe love was true.

She believed true love was accepting each other's
faults,
and always being there for you.

Through life's beautiful journeys and the trials
that come with time,
she believed true love was strong enough to last
the test of time.

Night of July

Cardinals that fly so effortlessly in the sunlit
sky,
to the bluebirds that are nesting their eggs in
the night of July.

From the night owls hooting their sovereign
cries,
to the brindled feathered hawks that encompass the
darkened night skies.

From dusk till dawn,
we hear the chirping songs of a world not yet
known.

That holds its mysteries like a fortune untold.

Divinely Guided

She always believed in fate not knowing
what it would bring,
but knowing God was never late made her
heart always sing.

For she knew he was always there every
step of the way,
leading and guiding her in his divinely
guided ways.

Garden of Eve

Rose petal blossoms in the Garden of Eve,
that blanket the floor with their quilt pattern
weave.

With the sweet and alluring fragrance of the day
lily blossoms.

To the tall, enchanted pillars,
that surround the garden's columns.

To the cascading white petals
of
the beautiful Magnolia.

Who is secretly as beautiful and as sweet,
as our skies golden novas.

To the sacred sentimental petals of the beautiful
Delilah,
that constantly flows like the rivers of
Italia.

God's Heart

When you are down on your luck,
and you don't think you can make it through.

Don't forget to look up,
because I have never forgotten you!

You mean more to me than
the stars, the moon, and the trees!

So why is it that you have so easily forgotten me?

Truly Free

If you know who you are,
you are truly free.

Just like the flowering blossoms
of a sugar orchard's humming bees.

Thy blossoms
never speak or have deliberate thoughts.

Yet,
they know the time is coming for them to
produce thy crops.

Thy bees are always busy gathering thy nectar of
life.

Humming with innocence and becoming bearers
of new life.

These things are truly simple,
yet so fascinating to see.
If you could only open your eyes,
You could truly see.

Star Gazing

The galaxies are so brisk,
hidden beyond the night's skies.

Even though we night gaze,
hoping to understand life.

We are truly so very simple and yet so very
small.

Entangled in this life's mysteries
and
stargazing at the night's skies in
awe.

Sand in the Hourglass

Always make time to enjoy your life.

For one day you'll blink,
and it'll have done passed you by.

Like sand in the hourglass
passing through.

Moments become distant memories.

Yet,
this is true.

Gifts of this Life

When you finally understand all of
life's most precious gifts.

You realize how short
life truly is.

The Apple Blossoms

As the apple blossoms bloom
with their appealing fragrance and allure.

The honey-blossom bees began to take flight
and stir.

Always in search of the sweetness and nectar of
life.

They are always humming with the melodies
and the precision of time.

As the apple blossoms bloom in full essence
waiting to be seen.

The honey blossom bees will soon begin their
stay,
gathering all the pollen until summer slowly
fades away.

Passion

True love is like a flame that burns so bright.

It ignites the passion throughout the
night.

Pages of Life

If your life were like the pages of an already-written book.

Would you ever go back and rewrite some of your pen ink strokes?

A Secret Garden

A secret garden with a fruitful essence,
brings forth beauty and an alluring presence.

Where time seems to stop
and
is an eternity long.

The sweet aroma of the blossoms
sing their gentle songs.

Will Love Unfold?

Love is never meant for more than
two souls.

For if a man is with more than one woman,
love can never unfold.

For if a man is with
two women
and
claims he loves both.

This is no more than a lie,
and
a false claim to boast.

"Dedication"

This book is dedicated to all our family, friends,

and everyone we hold dear to our hearts.

But mostly, this book is dedicated to

our

Lord and Savior,

Jesus Christ.

About the Authors

Linda Diane Lay, Angelia Richhart, and Amber Richhart are poets, writers, and authors of multiple great books. They reside in Indiana and have a love for poetry and the arts.

They have written an inspirational book named "Divinely Guided," which surrounds and entails the subjects of faith, love, hope, peace, and joy. While this book offers an inspirational message of love and acceptance through Jesus Christ, this book is based on Christianity and love. It is a good read for anyone wanting to learn more about Christianity, deepen their faith, and strengthen their relationship with Christ.

They have also written three poetic books that are anthologies, which are collections of poems from each author compiled together in one beautiful work, such as "The Sugar Orchard," "The Essence of a Pearl, and "Poetic Colors." These books dive deep into the depths of femininity and the emotions that women feel throughout life. Such as love, joy, and bliss, as well as exploring the sad poetic symphonies of pain, grief, and loss.

These books have words that will touch your heart and soul with beautifully drawn images to ignite your creativity. As well as words of wisdom, heartache, love, and grief that we have all felt throughout our lives. The words they use reflect such deep emotions that you will have cried the tears they have shed and shared the joy and feel as if you have encountered these life experiences yourself.

Linda Diane Lay, Angelia Richhart, and Amber Richhart use such passion and poetic expression when they write that the pages are engulfed in raw emotions. Anyone who reads their words from any of their poetic books can always relate to the emotions that they have felt.

www.ingramcontent.com/pod-product-compliance
Lightning Source LLC
Chambersburg PA
CBHW071240130726
47998CB00003B/1013